D1087856

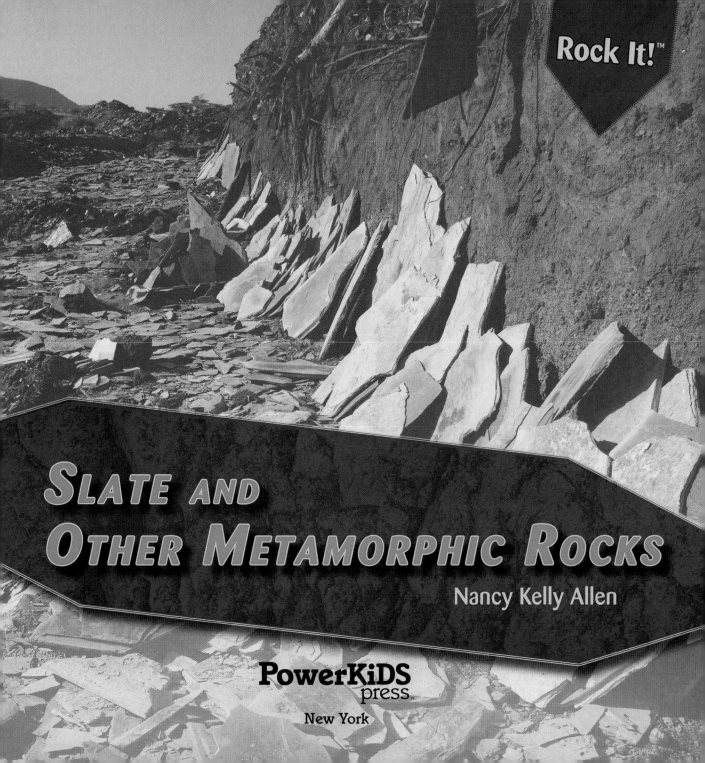

Rock It!™

Slate and Other Metamorphic Rocks

Nancy Kelly Allen

PowerKiDS press

New York

For Carly

Published in 2009 by The Rosen Publishing Group, Inc.
29 East 21st Street, New York, NY 10010

First Edition

Editor: Amelie von Zumbusch
Book Design: Kate Laczynski
Photo Researcher: Jessica Gerweck

Photo Credits: Cover, p. 1 © Randy Olson/Getty Images; pp. 4, 6, 10, 18, 20 Shutterstock.com; p. 8 © www.istockphoto.com/Melissa Carroll; p. 12 © www.istockphoto.com/Julien Grondin; p. 12 (inset) wikimedia commons; p. 14 © Dea Picture Library/Getty Images; p. 16 © www.istockphoto.com/David Woods.

Library of Congress Cataloging-in-Publication Data

Allen, Nancy Kelly, 1949–
    Slate and other metamorphic rocks / Nancy Kelly Allen. — 1st ed.
       p. cm. — (Rock it!)
    Includes index.
    ISBN 978-1-4358-2760-8 (library binding) — ISBN 978-1-4358-3183-4 (pbk.)
ISBN 978-1-4358-3189-6 (6-pack)
    1. Rocks, Metamorphic—Juvenile literature. I. Title.
    QE475.A2A45 2009
    552'.4—dc22
                                    2008033660

Manufactured in the United States of America

CONTENTS

The Heat Is On.. 5

Something Old Is New Again....................................... 7

Quite a Change.. 9

Crashing Plates 11

First One Rock and Then Another 13

Rock Changes... 15

Band Together 17

Rocks Without Bands... 19

Beautiful Nonfoliated Rocks.................................... 21

Cut It Out.. 22

Glossary... 23

Index.. 24

Web Sites... 24

Slate is sometimes used to make tiles, such as the ones covering the roofs of these houses in Dublin, Ireland. Slate roofs often last for over 100 years.

The Heat Is On

Earth is a huge mass made up of three kinds of rocks, called metamorphic rocks, igneous rocks, and sedimentary rocks. Can one kind of rock change into another? The answer is yes!

Metamorphic rocks form when heat and **pressure** produce changes in igneous rocks, sedimentary rocks, or other metamorphic rocks. For example, the metamorphic rock slate was once a sedimentary rock called shale. Metamorphic rocks generally form deep under ground. This is because the deeper a rock is buried underground, the more heat and pressure there is on it. Heat and pressure change the **properties** of existing rocks and turn them into metamorphic rocks.

Heat and pressure turn the sedimentary
rock shale (left) into the metamorphic rock slate
(right). Slate is much harder than shale is.

Something Old Is New Again

While sedimentary and igneous rocks can become metamorphic rocks, metamorphic rocks can become igneous or sedimentary rocks, too. Earth is always changing old rocks into new rocks. This pattern of changes is called the rock cycle.

Earth's crust, or outside **layer**, is made up of plates. Sometimes the plates crash together and produce heat and pressure inside Earth. Levels of pressure and **temperatures** even greater than those that create metamorphic rocks make rocks melt. Melted rock forms igneous rock when it hardens. Sedimentary rocks form when sediment, such as bits of rock worn away by wind and rain, pile into layers and harden into rock.

The mineral kyanite, seen here, is generally found in metamorphic rocks that formed under a lot of pressure.

Quite a Change

All rocks are made up of **minerals**. Minerals are natural matter that is not alive. Salt, gold, and diamonds are some well-known minerals. Some rocks are made of just one mineral, but most rocks have two or more minerals.

Sedimentary and igneous rocks become metamorphic rocks because heat and pressure cause the minerals in them to change. The new metamorphic rocks often have different properties from those of their parent rocks, or the rocks from which they formed. For example, the metamorphic rock marble is shinier than its parent rock, limestone.

The minerals in igneous and sedimentary rock begin to change when temperatures reach about 400° F (204° C). Higher temperatures produce greater changes in rocks.

The Andes are more than 8,000 miles (12,875 km) long. They reach from western Venezuela to southern Chile.

Crashing Plates

Metamorphic rocks form in several places. Some of these rocks form where Earth's plates rub together. You cannot feel the movement of plates on Earth's crust, but they are always moving slowly. When plates push against each other, lots of heat and pressure can build up. The heat and pressure change large areas of rock into metamorphic rock. This is called **regional** metamorphism.

Millions of years ago, crashing plates created the world's longest mountain range, the Andes, in South America. The Andes are mostly made up of the metamorphic rocks quartzite and slate, which formed through regional metamorphism. Today, heat and pressure inside the Andes continue to form new metamorphic rocks.

The heat of lava flowing over rocks can cause contact metamorphism. Inset: Hornfels forms by contact metamorphism inside Earth.

12

First One Rock and Then Another

Metamorphic rocks are also created when existing rocks get close to melted rock. Deep inside Earth, there are pockets of melted rock, or magma. Magma's heat bakes the rocks surrounding it. This changes the minerals in those rocks and turns them into metamorphic rocks. This is known as **contact** metamorphism. Bigger pockets of magma produce greater heat and change more rocks. The closer rocks are to hot magma, the more those rocks' minerals are changed by the heat.

Contact metamorphism takes place above ground, too. When magma flows out over Earth's **surface**, it is called lava. As lava flows over rocks, the rocks can become so hot that their minerals change.

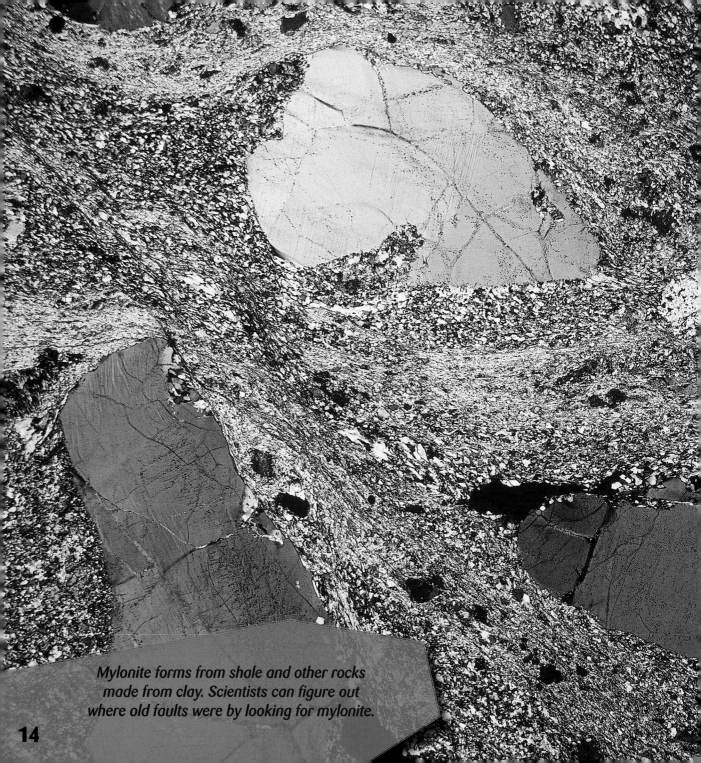

Mylonite forms from shale and other rocks made from clay. Scientists can figure out where old faults were by looking for mylonite.

Rock Changes

Dynamic metamorphism is another way that metamorphic rock forms. This happens at **earthquake** faults. Earthquake faults are breaks between Earth's plates where earthquakes take place. The pressure between the plates at a fault causes metamorphic rocks to form along the fault. For example, rocks called mylonites are created by layers of rock that moved along faults.

Metamorphic rocks can also form when certain liquids come into contact with rocks. These liquids add or take away some of the minerals in the rocks. The new metamorphic rocks that are created this way sometimes have metals, such as copper and lead, in them.

You can see the bands of color in this gneiss.
The rock is a piece of Lewisian gneiss, a kind
of gneiss that is about three billion years old.

Band Together

Have you ever seen rocks with stripes or wavy bands running through them? You may have been looking at **foliated** rocks. These are metamorphic rocks in which minerals form thin, flat layers that look like bands.

Many foliated rocks form from the sedimentary rock shale. The metamorphic rocks slate, phyllite, schist, and gneiss are all made from shale. Each of these rocks forms under a different amount of pressure and heat. When shale is under low heat and pressure, slate forms. Increasing amounts of heat and pressure form phyllite, then schist, and then gneiss.

Gems, or valued stones, called garnets can form when schist rocks are pressed together under high heat. Garnets are used to make earrings and necklaces. Most garnets are red, but they come in many colors.

Schools began using slate blackboards about 200 years ago. While most of today's classroom boards are made from other things, some slate boards are still used.

Rocks Without Bands

Have you ever seen rocks **sparkle**? Look closely at gneiss rocks. The minerals in these rocks, quartz, feldspar, and mica, actually sparkle. Some gneiss rocks were once igneous rocks, called granite. High heat and pressure flattened the granite's minerals and changed it into gneiss. The layers of minerals form light and dark bands in gneiss.

Slate forms layers, but it does not form bands of color. This gray rock has fine grains that break into thin sheets. Slate forms at low temperatures, so it sometimes still has **fossils** that its parent rock held.

Long ago, children did their schoolwork with chalk on pieces of dark gray slate. Today, flat, thin layers of slate are used to make pool tables.

The Taj Mahal, in Agra, India, is made of marble. This beautiful building was built as a memorial to the wife of Emperor Shah Jahan.

Beautiful Nonfoliated Rocks

Have you ever seen rocks that look like lumps of brown sugar? If you have, you likely saw quartzite. Quartzite is a sparkly metamorphic rock that forms from the sedimentary rock sandstone. Quartzite is a nonfoliated rock. Nonfoliated rocks are metamorphic rocks that have mineral grains that do not form bands.

Marble is another type of nonfoliated metamorphic rock. Marble forms from limestone, a sedimentary rock. Pure marble is white. However, small amounts of minerals in the limestone produce marble in colors such as red, green, gray, black, and pink.

The stone figure of President Abraham Lincoln at the Lincoln Memorial, in Washington, D.C., is made of 28 blocks of white marble and stands 19 feet (6 m) tall.

Cut It Out

Metamorphic rocks have many uses. Quartzite is used to make glass. Slate breaks easily into thin sheets, so it is often cut into tiles for roofs on houses. Slate tiles last through all types of weather. Marble is used in buildings because of its beauty and strength. Floors and walls are often made of marble. **Sculptors** enjoy working with marble because it is easy to cut, looks good, and will last for many years.

Metamorphic rock is hard, strong stone. This rock may have formed as a result of many changes, but the monuments and buildings made from it will last for centuries.

GLOSSARY

contact (KON-takt) Having to do with the touching or meeting of people or things.

earthquake (URTH-kwayk) A shaking of Earth caused by the movement of large pieces of land called plates that run into each other.

foliated (FOH-lee-ay-ted) Having to do with metamorphic rocks that include minerals in wavy lines or bands.

fossils (FO-sulz) The hardened remains of dead animals or plants.

layer (LAY-er) One thickness of something.

minerals (MIN-rulz) Natural things that are not animals, plants, or other living things.

pressure (PREH-shur) A force that pushes on something.

properties (PRAH-pur-teez) Features that belong to something.

regional (REEJ-nul) Having to do with a certain area.

sculptors (SKULP-turz) People who make art by shaping something, such as clay or stone.

sparkle (SPAHR-kul) To shine in quick flashes.

surface (SER-fes) The outside of anything.

temperatures (TEM-pur-cherz) How hot or cold things are.

INDEX

A
answer, 5

C
changes, 5, 7, 22
crust, 7, 11

E
Earth, 5, 7, 13

F
fault(s), 15
fossils, 19

G
ground, 5, 13

H
heat, 5, 7, 9, 11, 13, 17, 19

K
kinds, 5

L
layer(s), 7, 15, 17, 19

M
mass, 5
metamorphism, 11, 13, 15
mineral(s), 9, 13, 15, 19, 21

P
pattern, 7

plates, 7, 11, 15
pressure, 5, 7, 9, 11, 15, 17, 19
properties, 5, 9

R
rock cycle, 7

S
sculptors, 22
shale, 5, 17
surface, 13

T
temperatures, 7, 19

WEB SITES

Due to the changing nature of Internet links, PowerKids Press has developed an online list of Web sites related to the subject of this book. This site is updated regularly. Please use this link to access the list:
www.powerkidslinks.com/rockit/slate/